PETS PLUS

Birds

Sally Morgan

A⁺

Smart Apple Media

Published by Smart Apple Media, an imprint of Black Rabbit Books
P.O. Box 3263, Mankato, Minnesota 56002
www.blackrabbitbooks.com

Printed in the United States of America at Corporate Graphics, North Mankato, Minnesota

Published by arrangement with the Watts Publishing Group LTD, London.

Library of Congress Cataloging-in-Publication Data
 Morgan, Sally, 1957-
  Birds / Sally Morgan.
    p. cm. -- (Pets plus)
  Includes index.
  Summary: "Describes how to care for a pet bird, compares types of birds, and discusses wild bird behavior as compared to domestic birds in order to help readers decide if a bird is the right pet for them"--Provided by publisher.
  ISBN 978-1-59920-697-4 (library binding)
 1. Cage birds--Juvenile literature. I. Title.
 SF461.35.M67 2012
 636.6'8--dc23
                          2012000147

Created by Taglines Creative Ltd: www.taglinescreative.com
Author: Sally Morgan
Series designer: Hayley Cove
Editor: Jean Coppendale

Picture credits
t=top b=bottom l=left r=right m=middle
Front cover: logo, Gouldian finch, Shutterstock/Eric Isselée; feathers, Shutterstock/mjf99; top, wild budgerigars, Shutterstock/KKulikov; bottom, pet budgerigars, Shutterstock/Yuri Shirokov; Back cover: top, lorikeet, Shutterstock/Eric Isselée; bottom, house sparrow, Shutterstock/Vishnevskly Vasily; Title page: top, Shutterstock/Eric Isselée; Shutterstock/mjf99; left, parakeet, Ecoscene/Wayne Lawler; right, gray parrot, Ardea/John Daniels; Imprint page and top of spreads: house sparrow, Shutterstock/Vishnevskly Vasily; lorikeet, Shutterstock/Eric Isselée; p4l Ecoscene/Satyendra Tiwari, p4r Shutterstock/simon/naffarts; p5t Ardea/John Paul Ferrero, p5b Shutterstock/Rob Byron; p6t Shutterstock/Nicky Rhodes, p6b Shutterstock/Guido Akster; p7l Ecoscene/Angela Hampton, p7t Shutterstock/Katrina Brown; p8 Ecoscene/Angela Hampton; p9t Shutterstock/Theodore Scott, p9b Shutterstock/Jill Young; p10l Shutterstock/Rob Byron, p10r Shutterstock/Thomas Skjaeveland; p11l Shutterstock/ Ecoprint; p11r iStock/Nicola Stratford; p12 Ecoscene/Angela Hampton; p13t Ecoscene/Angela Hampton, p13b Ecoscene/Angela Hampton; p14 iStock/Sarah Bossert; p15t Shutterstock/Jasenka Luka, p15b Ecoscene/Angela Hampton; p16 iStock/ Webphotographer; p17l iStock/Glenn Jenkinson, p17r Shutterstock/Elena Elisseeva; p18 Ardea/Don Hadden; p19tl Shutterstock/Marina Jay, p19tm Shutterstock/Marina Jay, p19tr Shutterstock/Katrina Brown, p19b Shutterstock/Vishnevskly Vasily; p20l Shutterstock/Jill Lang, p20r Ecoscene/Fritz Polking; p21 Shutterstock/ Sarycheva Olesia; p22 Shutterstock/J van der Wolf; p23tl Ecoscene/Wayne Lawler, p23tr Ecoscene/Angela Hampton, p23b Ecoscene/Angela Hampton; p24l Ecoscene/ Sally Morgan, p24r Shutterstock/Borislav Borisov; p25 Shutterstock/Bernd Schmidt; p26l Shutterstock/Boris 15, p26r Shutterstock/Gorschkov; p27l Shutterstock/Pichugin Dimitry, p27tr Shutterstock/Nice Pictures, p27br Shutterstock/Christian Wilkinson; p29 Shutterstock/Jasenka Luka; p30 Shutterstock/Yuri Shirokov; p31 Shutterstock/K Kulikov; p32 Shutterstock/Elena Elisseeva

PO1436 / 2-2012

9 8 7 6 5 4 3 2 1

Contents

The meaning of the words in **bold** can be found in the glossary.

Pet Birds, Wild Birds

Pet birds, such as chickens and parrots, are closely related to their wild cousins. Birds are kept as pets for fun.

Wild Pets

People have kept birds for meat and eggs for thousands of years. Today, chickens living on farms and in yards have been bred from jungle fowl that lived in the **tropical** forests of Asia. Pet ducks and geese have wild cousins, too.

▼ This brightly colored male jungle fowl (below) is related to the tame chickens (right) that many people keep for eggs.

Pet Birds

Birds are kept as pets for many reasons. They may be kept for their sweet songs, their bright feathers, and as company. However, birds are not as **domesticated** as dogs and cats, and they need to be **tamed**.

Look Alike

The feathers of many pet birds are the same color as those of wild birds. For example, pet gray parrots look just like wild gray parrots.

However, some pet birds, such as parakeets, have been **bred** so that they have a bigger range of colors than wild birds.

▶ Wild parakeets (right) are mostly green, but pet parakeets (below) can be a variety of colors, including blue, yellow, and even white.

Birds as Pets

Birds make great pets. They can be friendly and chatty. Some love to play and learn tricks while others love to cuddle.

Cage or Aviary?

You can keep a pet bird in a cage in the house. As most cages are small, it is important to let a pet bird out to fly once a day in a closed room. Pet birds can be kept outside in an aviary, which is a bird house big enough for them to fly in. An **aviary** needs shelter from wind, rain, and sun, and a warm nest box for when it is cold.

▲ Many macaws have a **wingspan** of 40 inches (100 cm) or more, so the best place to keep a pet macaw (top) is in an outdoor aviary with plenty of space to fly, but these birds are not suitable for beginners.

Daily Care

Many small birds are easy to look after, but some of the more **exotic** birds need special diets and can catch diseases, which may result in high vet fees. Some birds, such as cockatoos, need lots of attention from their owner.

▶ Cockatoos are large, noisy birds that love company, but they are not suitable pets for beginners.

Buying Your Pet

If you buy your bird from a pet shop, make sure the birds look healthy and that their cages are clean. You can also buy birds from **breeders**. It is important to ask whether the animal was bred in **captivity**. Many exotic birds are caught in the wild and sold as pets, which threatens the survival of wild birds.

▲ Choose a bird that is suitable for a beginner, such as a parakeet or finch. A breeder can advise you about which type of bird to buy and how to care for it.

PET POINT

Many wild birds live in flocks in the wild and should not be kept alone. For example, canaries are best kept in pairs or small groups.

Which Bird?

From small finches to large macaws, there are many types of pet birds. Some species are easy to look after, but others require experience.

Large or Small?

Some people choose a large, colorful bird such as a parrot or macaw. These make great pets, but they are expensive to buy and may be very noisy. They need a big cage and can be messy. It is better to start off with small birds, such as canaries or lovebirds, that are cheaper and easier to care for.

Long Lives

When you are choosing your pet, remember that many birds have long lives. A macaw may live for 100 years or more. The African gray parrot can live up to 70 years, and a parakeet as many as 25 years.

◀ This African gray parrot has a large cage with lots of toys. It also has a perch outside of the cage so it can fly around the room.

Easy Care

Some birds, such as the colorful rainbow lorikeets, need a special diet of pollen and fruit. Because they produce runny droppings, their cages need a lot of cleaning. A better choice is a parakeet or a finch. These birds are very colorful, need less space than many other birds, and eat mostly common seeds.

▲ Zebra finches are easy to look after but should be kept in pairs.

Playful Parakeets

Some parakeets and parrots are very active. They love to play with toys. As these birds like to play with people and enjoy company, they would be happier in a home where people are around for most of the day.

◀ This eclectus parrot is having fun playing with its toys.

Your Bird's New Home

Before you bring your pet home, make sure its cage is placed somewhere safe and away from drafts and hot spots such as heat vents.

Large Cage

It is always best to buy the largest cage possible for your pet. At a minimum, the bird must be able to stretch its wings. If the cage has wire bars, make sure they are close together so your pet cannot push its head through them and get stuck. Place the cage where your pet can see people, but keep it away from windows, drafty areas, and banging doors.

Do It!

Checklist: Things you will need for your new pet:
- Cage and liner
- Food container
- Water bottle
- Toys, such as a mirror and bell
- Cuttlefish bone
- Perches
- Bird sand

▲ Parakeets should be let out of their cage to fly around at least once a day.

▲ Canaries in the wild (left) and the pet canary in its cage (right) use their sharp claws to grip on to a perch.

Bird Proof

Before you bring your bird home, make sure the room where you plan to keep it is safe. Flying birds may crash into windows and mirrors and get badly injured. Close the curtains before you let your bird out or put stickers on windows so your bird can see something is there. Mirrors need to be covered.

Perches

In the wild, many birds perch on branches to rest. Their toes wrap around the branch and grip so they don't fall off when they sleep. Make sure your bird's cage has perches of different sizes as this helps them to exercise their feet.

Caring for Your Pet

Keeping birds is easy as long as you follow a few basic rules to keep them happy, safe, and healthy.

Fresh Food and Water

Give your pet fresh food and water every day. Most birds prefer to drink from a water bottle rather than a bowl. Wash the bottle and food container every week.

PET POINT

Your pet bird may be scared of other pets, especially cats and dogs. Make sure these pets are out of the room when you clean your bird's cage or let it fly around out of its cage.

Snack Time

Sprays of **millet** are great snacks for your pet. Millet seeds are low in fat and will help to keep your pet healthy. Other healthy snacks include fruit such as apples.

◀ Regularly replace food treats, such as millet sticks, which birds like to peck.

Weekly Jobs

Each week, wipe the bars of the cage and clean out the tray at the bottom. Wash the **perches** and any toys. Every month, you need to remove your bird and give the cage a thorough cleaning. Always wash your hands after cleaning your bird's tray or cage.

▲ Give your pet some water in a solid, shallow bowl so it can enjoy a bath. Change this bath water every week.

Daily Job

Place a liner in the tray at the bottom of your bird's cage to catch its droppings. This needs to be changed daily so your pet does not have to walk in its own droppings. Be sure to wash your hands after changing the liner.

◄ Tray liners are made from sandpaper.

Handling Your Pet

You need to be able to handle your bird so you can easily move it in and out of its cage or take it to the vet.

Picking up Birds

Large birds are easier to pick up. Make sure you tuck in their wings and keep their head away from your face. Small birds are trickier to handle. You need to take some time to get your pet used to you before you handle it.

◀ Never hold a bird, such as this lovebird, around its chest as it will not be able to breathe.

Calming Talk

Birds get stressed easily. Talking to them helps calm them down. Talk to your bird, so it gets used to your voice. Next, give your pet a treat, so it gets used to your hand. Then you can start to handle your pet.

▶ Give your bird a treat, such as a piece of fruit, when you are training it.

Step Up!

Handling your bird is much easier if you train it to step on to your hand. Slowly extend your hand into its cage. Don't rush or your bird will get scared. Press your finger onto its belly just above its legs and it should step onto your finger. At the same time say "step up," and the bird will learn to do this.

◀ Your bird's feet and claws may feel a little scratchy at first, but you'll soon get used to them.

Health checks

A healthy bird has clean, shiny feathers, eats well, and is very active. Check your bird every day to make sure it is looking well.

Is My Bird Sick?

It is easy to tell if your bird is not well. It will sit at the bottom of its cage with its feathers **ruffled**. It may sneeze or have runny eyes and nostrils. It may make a **rasping** sound as it breathes. Droppings may be stuck to its tail feathers. If you think your pet is ill, tell an adult and take it to the vet for a checkup.

PET POINT

Some books tell people to use sandpaper perches to keep the bird's nails short. But this is more likely to cause sores on your pet's feet.

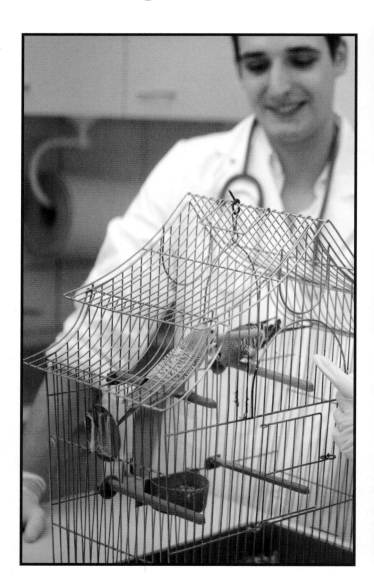

▲ Make sure your pet cannot escape on the way to see the vet. Take it in a cage or a small pet carrier.

Get a Trim

Some birds need their nails trimmed regularly. For example, parrots grow long nails that can be painful when they sit on your arm or shoulder.

Birds use their beaks to **preen** their feathers. If your bird's beak becomes overgrown or cracked, it needs to be trimmed. Take your bird to the vet for regular nail and beak trimming.

◀ A healthy bird, such as this Amazon parrot, has clean eyes, smooth feathers, a trimmed beak and nails, and looks alert.

▲ This rainbow lorikeet is using its beak to keep its feathers clean.

Life Cycle

When female birds lay eggs, some hatch into young birds called chicks. Parent birds care for their young until the chicks are ready to fly away.

▲ Parrots and parakeets, such as this red-fronted parakeet, build their nests in holes in trees.

Nest Building

Most wild birds build a nest in which to lay their eggs. Nests are made from materials, such as twigs and leaves, moss or mud, and lined with **downy** feathers. Pet birds make their nests in a nest box or on the floor of their cage.

Incubation

Female birds lay their eggs and then sit on them to keep them warm. This is called **incubation**. The chicks hatch a few weeks later. Many people collect the eggs from their pet birds and put them in an **incubator**. After they hatch, the chicks are fed by hand rather than by the parent birds.

Cockatiel Life Cycle

A female cockatiel is ready to breed at about a year old. She lays up to eight eggs, which hatch after three weeks. The chicks have a yellow-pink skin with few feathers. Both parents feed the chicks by coughing up food from their own stomachs. The chicks' eyes open after about 10 days. Their feathers grow quickly and they are able to fly by 5 weeks old. Their parents feed them until they learn to find food. The young birds leave their parents at about 3 months old. Cockatiels can live for about 20 years.

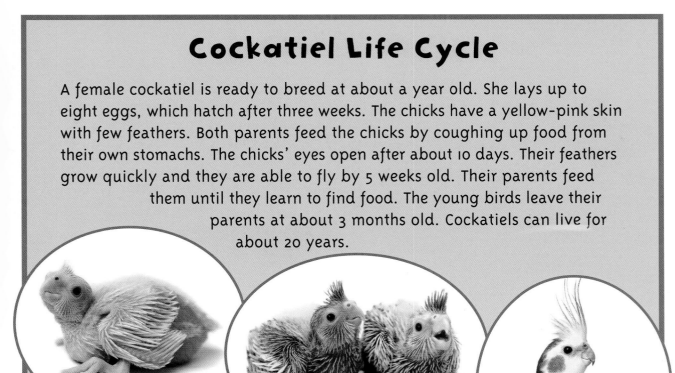

10-day-old chick

8-week-old chicks

young adult

Caring for Chicks

Birds are good parents and look after their chicks, protecting them and bringing them food. Some chicks are born naked and blind. Their parents keep them warm and feed them. Within a few weeks, the chicks have grown their feathers and are ready to leave the nest.

▶ Blackbirds catch worms, caterpillars, and small insects to feed their chicks.

Beaks and Food

A bird's beak is shaped to help it eat a certain type of food. You can tell what sort of food a bird eats by looking at its beak.

Seed Eaters

A seed-eating bird has a short, sturdy beak to crush tough seeds. Birds that are **predators**, such as owls and eagles, have a large, hooked beak to catch and hold prey. Hummingbirds and sunbirds have a long beak to reach into flowers. They use their long tongue to lap up the sugary **nectar**.

▲ The hyacinth macaw (above) uses its strong beak to crush palm fruits. These pet conures (left) have a similarly shaped beak that helps them to break open tough seeds and nuts.

Fruit and Veggies

Many people think pet birds eat only seeds, but most eat a mix of fruit, leafy vegetables, seeds, and even cheese and hard-boiled eggs. Wild birds love to eat fruit, just like their pet cousins.

PET POINT

Never feed your bird chocolate, avocado, apple seeds (the fruit is okay), tomatoes, or salt. These foods are bad for them.

◀ This parakeet is eating a variety of small seeds that it crushes and opens with its beak.

Ready-made Foods

Many different packaged foods are available for pet birds, and are prepared to suit a particular type or species. Often, food mixes contain added minerals and vitamins to make sure your bird stays healthy. Seedeaters, such as parakeets, canaries, and finches, need a mix of seeds each day, including millet and sunflower. It is best to buy a ready-made mix of seeds for your pet.

Wild Cousins

Pet birds may live in cages or aviaries, but they still have much in common with their wild cousins.

Living in a Flock

Many wild birds live in groups called flocks. A flock of birds stays together all the time. They fly and feed together to protect each other from predators. Most pet birds like company and need to be with other birds. They also enjoy being handled, and they like to play and be stroked.

▼ In Australia, it is common to see flocks of wild rainbow lorikeets in towns and gardens.

Keeping Busy

In the wild, birds spend a of lot time searching for food. Your pet will enjoy having toys to play with and food to "find," so hang some pieces of food in its cage. Make sure old food is cleaned out at the end of each day.

Sleeping in the Wild

Most birds are active during the day and sleep at night, except for a few **nocturnal** species, such as owls, that hunt at night. When it gets dark, birds **roost** in trees or creep into hollows in tree trunks. Pet birds also need to sleep at night. Some roost on their perches or sit on the cage floor.

▲ The wild monk parakeet (left) enjoys a tasty meal of fruit. The pet African gray parrot (right) found a peanut to eat.

▼ Many owners cover their pet's cage at night to keep out the light so the bird can sleep.

Bird Talk

Birds communicate with each other in many ways, but the most common is by using sound. Some have a sweet song—others a loud squawk!

Bird Song

Songbirds, such as blackbirds and skylarks, make the most amazing sounds. Male birds sing to tell other males that they are there and to attract females.

▼ Roosters (left) make a loud crowing noise, especially at dawn when they wake up. Robins (right) communicate with twitters, tweets, and songs.

Do It!

Some birds **mimic** words that they hear. If you want your pet to say something, speak the word clearly many times to encourage it to repeat.

▲ Mynah birds mimic human voices. Some pet birds can be taught words, sentences, and even songs.

Bird Calls

Birds that do not sing make calls instead. There are many types of calls, and each has a different meaning. Alarm calls alert other birds of danger. Birds call to each other when flying in a flock, and young chicks make peeps when they are calling out for their parents.

Talking Birds

Starlings are amazing mimics. They copy the song of other birds and other sounds, such as sheep and buses. Pet birds also can mimic the sounds that their owners make. The best pet mimic is the mynah bird. Others that are good at talking are parrots, macaws, and parakeets.

Instant Expert

There are about 10,000 species of birds in the world. Wild birds can be found in all **habitats** from jungles and deserts to the frozen **Arctic**.

The Biggest . . .

The tallest and biggest bird is the ostrich. It is so heavy that it cannot fly. The male can grow to 9 feet (2.74 m) in height and weigh 290 pounds (130 kg) or more. The females' eggs are huge and weigh approximately 3 pounds (1,500 g)—that's about the size of 28 chicken eggs.

► A chicken egg looks tiny next to the huge ostrich egg. The tiny ostrich chicks (far right) will soon grow into strong birds.

. . . and the Smallest

The male bee hummingbird is tiny. It is just 2 inches (5 cm) long and weighs only 0.06 oz. (1.8 g). It is found in Cuba.

The Fastest

The fastest bird is the peregrine falcon. It dives to catch its prey, reaching speeds of 200 miles per hour (322 km/h).

Extreme Fliers

The Arctic tern flies from the Arctic to the **Antarctic** and back every year—a distance of more than 23,600 miles (38,000 km). Some terns have flown up to 49,700 miles (80,000 km) in a year.

▲ Arctic terns fly long distances every year.

▲ Lovebirds are popular pets. They get their name from the way they behave. When they are kept in pairs, they sit close together and constantly groom each other.

FAST FACT

A small song bird, such as a robin, has about 4,000 feathers. A swan that lives in the Arctic has 25,000 feathers to help keep it warm.

▲ The wandering albatross spends most of its life flying over the ocean.

Largest Wingspan

The wandering albatross has the longest wingspan, at 12 feet (3.7 m) from tip to tip. Albatrosses are expert gliders, staying in the air for hours without beating their wings. They even sleep while they fly.

Pet Quiz

 Now that you know a bit more about what is involved in caring for birds, is a bird the right pet for you?

1. How often should your bird be allowed out of its cage?
   a) It doesn't need to be let out, because it has a big cage
   b) About once a week
   c) At least once a day

2. How long can a parakeet live?
   a) Not very long
   b) About 5 years
   c) About 25 years

3. How big should your bird's cage be?
   a) Not very big
   b) Just larger than the bird
   c) Big enough so it can spread its wings

4. If you see your pet bird sitting on the floor of its cage with its feathers ruffled, it is:
   a) Sleeping
   b) Resting
   c) Unwell

5. How much time do you have to spend with your pet each day?
   a) Not much, I'm very busy
   b) I can spend lots of time with it on weekends
   c) I'll spend some time with it every day

Pet Quiz Results

If you answered **(c)** to most of the questions, a bird could be a pet for you.

Owning a Pet: Checklist

All pets need to be treated with respect. Remember your pet bird can feel pain and distress.

To be a good pet owner, you should remember these five rules. Make sure your pet:

- never suffers from fear and distress
- is never hungry or thirsty
- never suffers discomfort
- is free from pain, injury, and disease
- and has freedom to show its normal behavior

To keep your pet healthy and happy, you have to check it at least twice a day to make sure it has enough fresh water and food.

You must remember to buy new supplies of its food in time so that your pet never goes hungry.

You must keep your bird's cage or aviary clean. Check its cage or aviary to make sure there is nothing there that

may hurt it and that it cannot escape. Also, make sure no other pets or animals can harm or scare your bird.

Make sure your pet's cage is not in direct sunlight or above a heat vent. Do not keep the cage next to a noisy radio or television.

Your bird must have enough space to fly, and it should be allowed to fly out of its cage at least once a day for about an hour. Make sure that rooms are made bird-safe before letting your pet fly indoors.

If your pet bird becomes ill or hurts itself, tell an adult and take your pet to be checked by a vet.

Glossary

Antarctic the region around the South Pole

Arctic the region around the North Pole

aviary a huge space with shelter, usually outdoors, where many birds are kept and where they can fly around

bred the careful selection of parents to produce young with special features

breeder a person who keeps animals, such as a pet birds, to breed and sell

captivity when wild animals are kept in places such as parks or zoos and are not free to roam in their natural habitat

domesticated tamed and used to living with people

downy soft and fluffy

exotic strange, unusual, from a different part of the world

habitats the surroundings or places in which animals live

incubation keeping an egg or young warm so it will develop and grow

incubator a device that is used to hatch eggs by keeping them warm

millet a type of grain, such as wheat and oats

mimic to copy and imitate

nectar a sugary liquid produced by some flowers

nocturnal active at night

perch (verb) to rest on a branch; (noun) a branch that a bird uses to rest on

predator an animal that hunts and eats other animals

preen to clean and smooth the feathers with the beak

rasping a scraping sound

roost when a bird rests for the night

ruffled when feathers are out of place or roughed up

tamed no longer wild

tropical part of the world near the equator where the climate is hot and wet

wingspan the distance from one wingtip to the other

Websites

Get ASPCA's tips on caring for your pet bird.
http://www.aspca.org/Home/ASPCAKids/Pet-Care/bird-care.aspx

Click on "Birds" to learn about birds in the wild.
http://kids.nationalgeographic.com/kids/animals/creaturefeature/

Find bird facts and activities at Enchanted Learning.
http://www.enchantedlearning.com/subjects/birds/

Index

DATE DUE

AUG 27 2013

PRINTED IN U.S.A.